TAKE THE LEAD

CLARINET

HUGE HITS

Editorial, production and recording: Artemis Music Limited • Design and production: Space DPS Limited • Published 2003

RESPECT
THE VALUE OF
MUSIC

IMP

International
MUSIC
Publications

Anything Is Possible

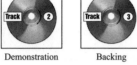

Demonstration   Backing

Words and Music by
Cathy Dennis and Chris Braide

Come Away With Me

Demonstration   Backing

Words and Music by Norah Jones

Come Undone

Demonstration

Backing

Words and Music by
Robert Williams, Daniel Pierre,
Ashley Hamilton and Pierre Ottestad

Cry Me A River

Demonstration

Backing

Words and Music by Timothy Mosley,
Scott Storch and Justin Timberlake

Hero

Demonstration   Backing

Words and Music by Enrique Iglesias,
Paul Barry and Mark Taylor

On The Horizon

Demonstration

Backing

Words and Music by Gregg Alexander,
Richard Nowels and Melanie Chisholm

Medium pop tempo

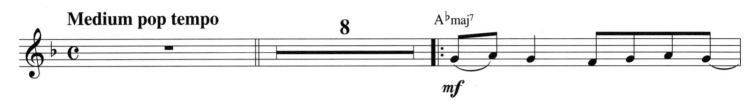

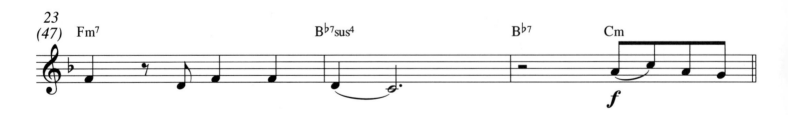

Sound Of The Underground

Demonstration

Backing

Words and Music by Brian Higgins,
Niara Scarlett and Miranda Cooper

Spirit In The Sky

Demonstration

Backing

Words and Music by Norman Greenbaum

YOU'RE THE VOICE

8861A PV/CD

Casta Diva from Norma – Vissi D'arte from Tosca – Un Bel Di Vedremo from Madama Butterfly – Addio, Del Passato from La Traviata – J'ai Perdu Mon Eurydice from Orphee Et Eurydice – Les Tringles Des Sistres Tintaient from Carmen – Porgi Amor from Le Nozze Di Figaro – Ave Maria from Otello

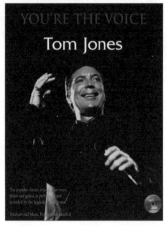

8860A PVG/CD

Delilah – Green Green Grass Of Home – Help Yourself – I'll Never Fall In Love Again – It's Not Unusual – Mama Told Me Not To Come – Sexbomb – Thunderball – What's New Pussycat – You Can Leave Your Hat On

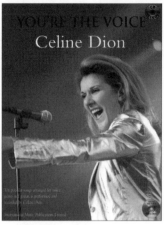

9297A PVG/CD

Beauty And The Beast – Because You Loved Me – Falling Into You – The First Time Ever I Saw Your Face – It's All Coming Back To Me Now – Misled – My Heart Will Go On – The Power Of Love – Think Twice – When I Fall In Love

9349A PVG/CD

Chain Of Fools – A Deeper Love Do Right Woman, Do Right Man – I Knew You Were Waiting (For Me) – I Never Loved A Man (The Way I Loved You) – I Say A Little Prayer – Respect – Think – Who's Zooming Who – (You Make Me Feel Like) A Natural Woman

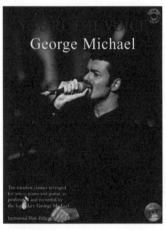

9007A PVG/CD

Careless Whisper – A Different Corner – Faith – Father Figure – Freedom '90 – I'm Your Man – I Knew You Were Waiting (For Me) – Jesus To A Child – Older – Outside

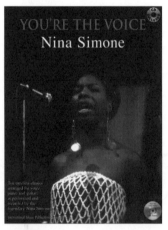

9606A PVG/CD

Don't Let Me Be Misunderstood – Feeling Good – I Loves You Porgy – I Put A Spell On You – Love Me Or Leave Me – Mood Indigo – My Baby Just Cares For Me – Ne Me Quitte Pas (If You Go Away) – Nobody Knows You When You're Down And Out – Take Me To The Water

9700A PVG/CD

Beautiful – Crying In The Rain – I Feel The Earth Move – It's Too Late – (You Make Me Feel Like) A Natural Woman – So Far Away – Way Over Yonder – Where You Lead – Will You Love Me Tomorrow – You've Got A Friend

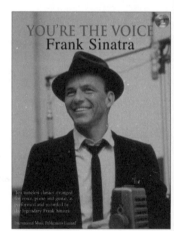

9746A PVG/CD

April In Paris – Come Rain Or Come Shine – Fly Me To The Moon (In Other Words) – I've Got You Under My Skin – The Lady Is A Tramp – My Kinda Town (Chicago Is) – My Way – Theme From *New York, New York* – Someone To Watch Over Me – Something Stupid

9770A PVG/CD

Cry Me A River – Evergreen (A Star Is Born) – Happy Days Are Here Again – I've Dreamed Of You – Memory – My Heart Belongs To Me – On A Clear Day (You Can See Forever) – Someday My Prince Will Come – Tell Him (duet with Celine Dion) – The Way We Were

9799A PVG/CD

Boogie Woogie Bugle Boy – Chapel Of Love – Friends – From A Distance – Hello In There – One For My Baby (And One More For The Road) – Only In Miami – The Rose – When A Man Loves A Woman – Wind Beneath My Wings

9810A PVG/CD

Ain't No Sunshine – Autumn Leaves – How Can I Keep From Singing – Imagine – It Doesn't Matter Anymore – Over The Rainbow – Penny To My Name – People Get Ready – Wayfaring Stranger – What A Wonderful World

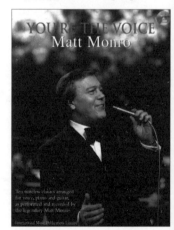

9889A PVG/CD

Around The World – Born Free – From Russia With Love – Gonna Build A Mountain – The Impossible Dream – My Kind Of Girl – On A Clear Day You Can See Forever – Portrait Of My Love – Softly As I Leave You – Walk Away

The outstanding vocal series from IMP

CD contains full backings for each song, professionally arranged to recreate the sounds of the original recording

Karaoke Classics
9696A   PVG/CD
ISBN: 1-84328-202-X

Back For Good – Delilah – Hey
Baby – I Will Always Love You –
I Will Survive – Let Me Entertain
You – Reach – New York, New
York – Summer Nights – Wild
Thing

Party Hits
9499A   PVG/CD
ISBN: 1-84328-097-3

Come On Eileen – Dancing
Queen – Groove Is In The Heart
– Hi Ho Silver Lining – Holiday –
House Of Fun – The Loco-
Motion – Love Shack – Staying
Alive – Walking On Sunshine

Disco
9493A   PVG/CD
ISBN: 1-84328-091-4

I Feel Love – I Will Survive – I'm
So Excited – Lady Marmalade –
Le Freak – Never Can Say
Goodbye – On The Radio –
Relight My Fire – YMCA – You
Sexy Thing

Celebration Songs
9733A   PVG/CD
ISBN: 1-84328-241-0

Anniversary Waltz - Auld Lang
Syne – Celebration –
Congratulations - God Save
The Queen - Happy Birthday -
Happy Birthday To You - My
Way - The Best - We Are The
Champions

Tear-Jerkers
9803A   PVG/CD
ISBN: 1-84328-326-3

The First Time Ever I Saw Your
Face – Hello – If You Don't
Know Me By Now – It's My
Party – Stay With Me Till Dawn
– The Way We Were - What
Becomes Of The Broken
Hearted – When A Man Loves
A Woman – When I Need You –
Will You Love Me Tomorrow

One-Hit Wonders
9843A   PVG/CD
ISBN: 1-84328-396-4

Breakfast At Tiffany's – Can You
Dig It – I'll Be There For You –
Imagination – It's Raining Men –
Macarena – Runaway Train –
Something In The Air – Spirit In
The Sky – Would I Lie To You

 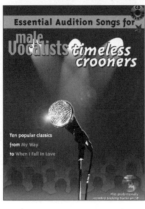   

ESSENTIAL AUDITION SONGS FOR FEMALE VOCALISTS

Broadway
7171A   Book and CD   ISBN: 1859098010

Anything Goes – As Long As He Needs Me – Being Alive – But Not For Me – Fifty Percent – Johnny One Note – Nothing – People – Take Me Or Leave Me – There Won't Be Trumpets

Jazz Standards
7021A   Book and CD   ISBN: 1859097529

Cry Me A River – Desafinado– Ev'ry Time We Say Goodbye – Fever – It's Only A Paper Moon – Mad About The Boy – My Baby Just Cares For Me – Stormy Weather (Keeps Rainin' All The Time) – Summertime – They Can't Take That Away From Me

Pop Ballads
6939A   Book and CD   ISBN: 185909712X

Anything For You – Do You Know Where You're Going To – I Will Always Love You – Killing Me Softly With His Song – My Heart Will Go On – Over The Rainbow – Promise Me – The Greatest Love Of All– The Way We Were– Walk On By

Pop Divas
7769A   Book and CD   ISBN: 1859099874

Beautiful Stranger – Believe – Genie In A Bottle – I Don't Want To Wait – I Try – Pure Shores – The Greatest Love Of All – Un-Break My Heart – Waiting For Tonight – Without You

ESSENTIAL AUDITION SONGS FOR MALE VOCALISTS

Broadway
9185A   Book and CD   ISBN: 1843280124

Don't Get Around Much Anymore From Sophisticated Ladies – Get Me To The Church On Time From My Fair Lady – If I Were A Rich Man From Fiddler On The Roof – It Don't Mean A Thing (If It Ain't Got That Swing) From Sophisticated Ladies – It's All Right With Me From Can–Can – On The Street Where You Live From My Fair Lady – Thank Heaven For Little Girls From Gigi – The Lady Is A Tramp From Babes In Arms – Wandrin' Star From Paint Your Wagon – With A Little Bit Of Luck From My Fair Lady

Timeless Crooners
9495A   Book and CD   ISBN: 1843280922

Can't Take My Eyes Off You – I Left My Heart In San Francisco – Mack The Knife – My Way – Swingin' On A Star – The Way We Were – Theme From 'New York, New York' – (What A) Wonderful World – When I Fall In Love – Volare

ESSENTIAL AUDITION SONGS FOR MALE & FEMALE VOCALISTS

Duets
7432A   Book and CD   ISBN: 1859099009

Barcelona – Don't Go Breaking My Heart – Endless Love – I Got You Babe – I Knew You Were Waiting (For Me) – (I've Had) The Time Of My Life – It Takes Two – Kids – Nothing's Gonna Stop Us Now – Summer Nights

Kids
7341A   Book and CD   ISBN: 1859098673

Bugsy Malone – Consider Yourself – Love's Got A Hold On My Heart – Maybe This Time – My Favourite Things – My Name Is Tallulah – Over The Rainbow – We're In The Money – Wouldn't It Be Loverly – You're Never Fully Dressed Without A Smile

Wannabe Pop Stars
9735A   Book and CD   ISBN: 1843282453

Angels – Anything Is Possible – Back For Good – Ev'ry Time We Say Goodbye – Flying Without Wings – Genie In A Bottle – Get Happy – Reach – Up On The Roof – Whole Again

Love Songs
9841A   Book and CD   ISBN: 1843283905

Amazed – Embraceable You – The First Time Ever I Saw Your Face – Get Here – I Turn To You – Kiss Me – Let's Stay Together – Save The Best For Last – Saving All My Love For You – You Don't Have To Say You Love Me